Enter here!

T0359228

This year you will be enteri... worlds of FLUENCY and LE...

You will practise writing faster usin... the joins including some special new ones.

You will develop a writing style that is easily read by others.

JOB APPLICATION: HANDWRITING EXPLORER

Name: _____

Date of birth: _____

Previous handwriting experience: _____

_____

_____

Why I would make a good handwriting explorer:

_____

_____

Trace then write the anticlockwise letters.

a   c   d   g   q

o   e   f   s

Trace then write the clockwise letters.

m   n   r   x   z

h   k   p

Trace then write the i family letters.

l   t   i   j

Trace then write the u family letters.

u   y   v   w   b

Practise capital letters.

z z Z Z Z Z

Trace.

A B C D E F G H I J K L M

N O P Q R S T U V W X Y Z

Handwriting: review letter families; review lower case and capital letters.

To link to a, c, d, g and q, lift your pencil and drop them on to the exit of the letter in front.

u → u → u → u·a

Make an exit . . . keep going up . . . then lift your pencil and drop-in the letter.

lift pencil here

Trace the letter pairs.

ma ma na na uc ic ud id ca da ma na

ug ig ug ig ng nd nc ta ca da ng nd sq

ta ta ta ha ha ka ka td ad ac ta ta sa

Trace then write.

mad sad dad madly gladly

squiggle giggle ring sing sting

later alligator elder adder

Handwriting: touch joins. **Grammar:** adverbs (madly, gladly). **Spelling and vocabulary:** common letter pairs; rhyme.

Lift your pencil when you make a horizontal touch join.

lift pencil here

wa

Trace then write.

wa ba fa od rg va oc rc ra rd

Trace then write.

awake fake large sergeant archway

apology technology archaeology

A pen lift means your hand can take a little break before you drop in the next letter.

Trace then write.

The ugly duckling turned into a swan.

That's a cygnet!

Self-assessment   Circle your five best joins on the page.

Handwriting: touch joins. **Punctuation:** sentence punctuation. **Spelling and vocabulary:** common letter pairs; animal young (ducklings, cygnet). **Literary elements:** references to fairy tale ('The Ugly Duckling', Hans Christian Andersen).

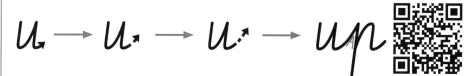

A diagonal join links to the next letter at the top of that letter's body.

$u \rightarrow u \rightarrow u \rightarrow up$

Make an   then keep going up . . .   until you get to the
exit . . .   start of the next letter.

Trace then write. Remember to make smooth diagonal joins.

ar ai aj am an au av aw ay

ap cr ce cu dr du di ei ey

ep eu em en er ew ee hi he

hu hy in im er ki ke kn ky

kr mn mi mu mm my mp ni

ny nu nn ui uy up ur um un

Self-assessment   Circle your smoothest join.
Underline a join that needs more practice.

Handwriting: diagonal joins to body and to body and tail letters (descenders). **Spelling**: common letter pairs.

u → *u* → *u* → *u* *u* *ul*

*Make an   keep going up . . . to the very top . . . then retrace to make
exit . . .   the next letter.*

To connect a diagonal join to a tall head and body letter, continue the exit all the way up to the top, then retrace to make the next letter.

Trace then write. Be careful when you retrace the join.

al   ah   al   ak   at   cl   ch   ck

ct   dt   dl   dh   el   et   eb   ht

ht   ik   il   it   ib   kl   kh   ll   lk   kl

lt   mb   ml   nb   nh   nt   nk   nl   nl

th   tt   tl   uk   ub   ut   ul   at   it   th

pick of the litter

Pick me!

Self-assessment *My retracing to make joins is:
improving ☐ good ☐ fantastic ☐.*

Handwriting: diagonal joins to head and body letters (ascenders). Spelling: common letter pairs. Literary elements: idiom.

u → u → uf → uf

Go up . . .   to the   then make   Lift your pencil
           top body line . . .   a loop.   and add the crossbar.

Trace then write.

uf uf   uf uf
ef ef   if if
af af   df df

Trace then write.

loafing swift drift dreadful unsafe

boxfish wolf oaf elf waif chief shelf

The three pigs fled

from the oafish wolf.

Self-assessment   My loops to join f are smooth and fluent:
                   sometimes ☐ often ☐ always ☐.

Handwriting: diagonal joins to f. **Grammar**: adjectives; nouns; verbs. **Spelling and vocabulary**: common letter pairs. **Literary elements**: reference to folk tale ('The Three Pigs').

Make a diagonal exit . . .   and swing around smoothly to x.   Lift your pencil and form the second stroke of x.

Trace then write.

ax ax ax ax ax ax ax ax ax ax

ux ux ux ux ux ux ux ux ux ux

ix ix ix ix ix ix ix ix ix ix ix ix ix

ex ex ex ex ex ex ex ex ex ex ex ex ex

mix fix fax flux flex six saxophone

pixie pixels flax exit tuxedo exhale

Self-assessment

Put a cross next to any joins to x that you could improve.

Handwriting: diagonal joins to x. **Spelling and vocabulary**: x says 'ks' in each word on this page.

Use a diagonal join to join from q to u.

q → q → q/ → qu

Continue the exit all the way up to the top body line.

Trace then write.

qu qu qu qu qu qu qu qu

qu qu qu qu qu qu qu

The quick queen queued for quoits.

The quirky quokkas quested for quiche.

Write your own words that have a qu.

Handwriting: diagonal join from q to u. Spelling: common letter pairs. Literary elements: alliteration.

9

To make a faster diagonal join to s, change the shape of the s.

a → *a* → *as*

top of s is much shorter

Make a diagonal exit kick ...

keep going to make a short top on the s ...

then quickly retrace around.

Trace then write.

as as as as as as as as as as as

is is is is is is is is is is is is

ns ns ns ns ns ns ns ns ns ns ns

ts ts ts ts ts ts ts ts ts ts ts ts

ts ts ts ts ts ts ts ts ts ts ts ts ts

To make a diagonal join from s, you need to retrace.

retrace *sk*

Retrace the bottom of the s.

ask
retrace

Then go up to make a diagonal join.

Trace then write.

si su sn st so st

Handwriting: diagonal joins to and from s.

10

Practise diagonal joins with these plurals. Trace then write.

snakes lizards walruses kisses prizes

batteries apologies activities dragonflies

loaves thieves knives

hooves elves calves

Remember to pause if you need to and relax your hold on the pen or pencil.

Trace then write.

"The time has come," the Walrus said,

"To talk of many things:

Of shoes — and ships — and sealing-wax

Of cabbages — and kings."

Handwriting: diagonal joins to and from s. **Punctuation:** sentence punctuation, speech marks. **Spelling and vocabulary:** plurals adding -s, -es, -ies. **Literary elements:** quote from *Through the Looking Glass*, by Lewis Carroll (1872).

by or ry

A horizontal join is a line with a little wave.

> To join from a letter that finishes near the top body line, you need a horizontal join.

Trace then write.

oy on on om oz oi ow on on

ry rn ru rm ru ri rr rp ru

vy vu vi vr vu vi by bi bu ba bo br

wi wr wu wy wi wr wu wy wn wo

Trace then write the similes.

burps like a yowie

wriggles like a viper

BURP

wriggle wriggle

Circle your five best horizontal joins.

Handwriting: horizontal joins from letters that finish near the top body line (b, o, r, v, w). **Spelling:** digraph 'ur' (burp); digraph 'ow' (yowie).
Literary elements: similes.

To make a horizontal join to e, you need to dip down.

be be dip

To join e, dip down.

Trace then write.

oe re ve we be oe re ve we be

oe re ve we be oe re ve we be

believe deceive receive leave heave

we're were does doesn't have haven't

"The werewolf doesn't exist,"

remarked the man.

The werewolf doesn't exist.

Huh!

Handwriting: Horizontal joins to e from o, r, v, w, b. **Punctuation:** sentence punctuation; speech marks. **Grammar:** verbs. **Spelling and vocabulary:** apostrophes for contractions (we're, doesn't, haven't). **Literary elements:** reference to *The Bunyip of Berkeley's Creek;* by Jenny Wagner and illustrated by Ron Brooks (1973).

Practise horizontal joins to e. Remember to pause if you need to and relax your hold on the pen or pencil.

Trace then write.

oe re ve we be oe re ve we be

Trace then write these adverbs.

carefully incredibly agreeably beadily

entirely vertically reliably readily

bravely cleverly greedily prettily

dreadfully drearily dreamily weekly

Write some sentences using the adverbs above.

Handwriting: horizontal joins to e from o, r, v, w, b. **Grammar:** how adverbs ending in -ly, add -ly to change adjectives to adverbs (careful/carefully, incredible/incredibly). **Spelling and vocabulary:** change y to i to add ly (greedy/greedily); double final l before adding ly (dreadful/dreadfully).

Trace then write the words to practise joins to e.

foe goes volcanoes tomatoes heroes woeful

whoever wrongdoer does joey answer

cobwebs welcome weary superpower

allowed sweaty tower webbed forgive

above clever government curve forever

develop never paperweight

address admire firefighter

adventure breeze derelict

Self-assessment Underline any horizontal joins to e that you could improve.

Handwriting: horizontal joins to e from o, r, v, w, b. **Spelling and vocabulary:** compound words (firefighter, paperweight), add –es to words that end in o to make plural.

$u \rightarrow u' \rightarrow u\cdot l \rightarrow wh$

From the exit . . . go up . . . then retrace down.

To join a letter that finishes near the top body line to a head and body letter, you need to retrace.

Trace then write.

ob oh ok ol bl rk rb rl wh ot

howl hoot spooky weird blowing

whirl swirl dark disturbing fearless

Trace then write.

It was very dark and the wind

howled horribly around her.

Self-assessment

Circle your five best horizontal joins.

Handwriting: horizontal joins to head and body letters (ascenders) b, h, k, l, t. **Grammar:** adjectives (spooky, weird, dark); adverb (horribly).
Spelling and vocabulary: digraphs 'ow', 'oo', 'ir', 'ur', 'ar'. **Literary elements:** alliteration (howled horribly); fantasy settings/scary genre; quote from *The Wonderful Wizard of Oz*, by L Frank Baum (1900).

To make a horizontal join to f, use a loop.

σ → of → of

Go across . . .

then make a loop.

Lift your pencil and make a loop.

Trace then write.

of bf rf wf of bf rf wf of

of often roof proof soft loft

awful snowfall perfume starfish

Join from f at the crossbar.

To make a double f, swing the first crossbar up to make the second loop.

horizontal join at crossbar

fr fs fe fi

off

Trace then write.

fa fi fo fu fr fs fy fl fe

fly flip flop flash flow flame

Handwriting: horizontal joins to and from f; joining from the crossbar; double f. **Grammar**: verbs; adjectives.

17

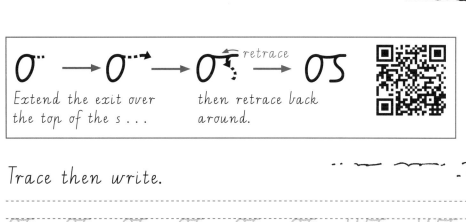

To make a horizontal join
from s, retrace the top of the s.

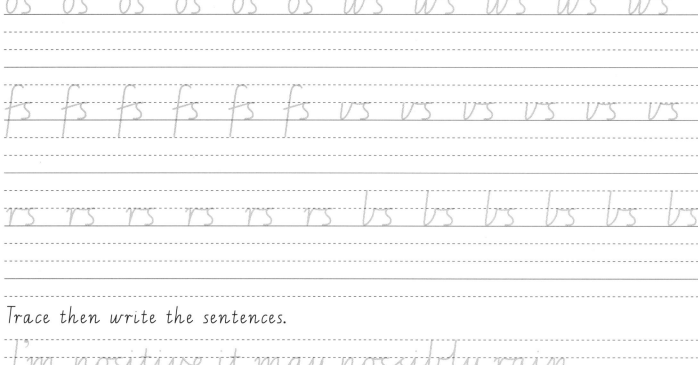

Extend the exit over
the top of the s . . .

then retrace back
around.

Trace then write.

os os os os os os ws ws ws ws ws

fs fs fs fs fs fs vs vs vs vs vs vs

rs rs rs rs rs rs bs bs bs bs bs bs

Trace then write the sentences.

I'm positive it may possibly rain.

The oafs wore scarfs and briefs.

Self-assessment   Tick any joins to s that are excellent.
Underline any joins that you could improve.

Handwriting: horizontal joins to s. **Grammar:** modality (positive, possibly).

Remember to use your non-writing hand to keep the paper in position. Make sure your writing arm and hand can move freely.

Trace then write.

pianos banjos solos cellos sopranos

mangos avocados autos kangaroos

roofs dwarfs beliefs cliffs castoffs

advisors cleaners managers smugglers

moss post whose nose utmost rose

sniffs snuffs whiffs hoofs bluffs

course coarse thirst first juniors

Handwriting: horizontal joins to s. **Spelling and vocabulary**: homophones (course/coarse); musical terms ending in o just add 's' (pianos); jobs often end in 'er', 'or' or 'ist' (advisors, cleaners).

19

g, j, y and z are letters that have a tail pointing to the left. They don't join to the next letter, yet.

We'll teach you how to join them later.

Trace then write the adjectives. Notice the letters that aren't joined.

agile amazing glowing gentle green

giggly jiggly gaudy jaunty jealous

juicy jagged jovial pongy pungent

prized saggy shaggy yellow yoghurty

yummy yucky zany zesty

Write a sentence of your own. Use adjectives from above.

Handwriting: letters that have a tail pointing to the left (g, j, y, z) don't join yet. **Grammar:** adjectives; sentences. **Spelling and vocabulary:** rhyme (jiggly/giggly, saggy/shaggy).

Trace then write the compound words.

cubbyhouse stepping stone eggshell

piggyback grasshopper passionfruit

Trace then write.

Out of the smoggy city, across the

choppy sea, over the rugged mountains,

down the slippery slope, into the

pebbly stream, through the grassy

field, for an apple.

Handwriting: double letters. **Punctuation:** commas to separate phrases. **Grammar:** prepositional phrases; adjectives; common nouns; prepositions. **Spelling and vocabulary:** compound words.

Review: Double letters

Trace then write.

cc

dd

oo

ll

mm

ee

rr

tt

ff

Practise joining these double letters. Remember that tt has a double crossbar.

Trace then write.

accepting adding stooping pulling

humming running sleeping slurring

hitting puffing slipping getting

Self-assessment

Underline any joins that you could improve.

Handwriting: double letters. **Grammar:** verbs; tense. **Spelling and vocabulary:** double final consonant to add -ing (hit/hitting, run/running).

22

Trace then write these compound words.

overall wallpaper overrun waterproof

strawberry rattlesnake toadstool

kneecap seagull foolproof toothbrush

Trace then write the similes.

A cat's purr is beautiful,

like a strange lullaby.

Prrrrrr . . . Prrrrrr . . .

A cat's purr feels

like a car's motor running.

Handwriting: double letters. **Grammar:** possessive apostrophes (cat's, car's). **Punctuation:** ellipsis (. . .). **Spelling and vocabulary:** compound words. **Literary elements:** similes; quote from *The Five Lives of our Cat Zook*, by Joanne Rocklin (2012).

A **palindrome** is a word, phrase or sentence that reads the same forwards or backwards.

Trace the palindrome words.

bib	dad	deed
did	dud	eve
eye	gag	gig
kayak	level	madam
mum	nan	noon
peep	pip	pop
pup	radar	redder

Trace the palindrome phrases and sentences. Then try writing some palindromes of your own.

race car   swap paws

snack cans   stunt nuts

Too bad I hid a boot.

Race fast, safe car.

Self-assessment   Tick your best joins.
Put a cross next to any joins that need more practice.

Handwriting: fluency and legibility; all joins. **Grammar**: sentences. **Literary elements**: palindromes.

Trace then write these words that are often misspelt. How fast can you write them without making any spelling mistakes and still be neat?

Remember, keep your pencil hold relaxed and flexible.

about	almost
always	answer
because	before
cannot	clothes
coming	doctor
doesn't	eighth
enough	except
excited	friend
guess	having
heard	know
laugh	might
often	people

Don't lose those loose wheels.

Self-assessment   Circle five words that show your writing is fluent and legible.

Handwriting: fluency and legibility; all joins. **Spelling and vocabulary**: frequently misspelt words.

Remember to sit comfortably and make sure your writing hand and arm can move freely.

Trace then write each adjective to describe how something **looks**.

grotesque multicoloured crooked dirty

Trace then write each adjective to describe how something **sounds**.

blaring hushed squeaking raspy loud

Trace then write each adjective to describe how something **tastes**.

bitter delicious sour yummy tangy

Trace then write each adjective to describe how something **smells**.

perfumed putrid noxious musty burnt

Trace then write each adjective to describe how something **feels**.

fluffy fuzzy prickly damp slippery

Write your own adjectives to describe how something looks, sounds, tastes, smells or feels.

Handwriting: fluency and legibility; all joins. **Grammar**: adjectives. **Literary elements**: descriptions that make use of senses.

Trace then write the different ways to say 'said'.

announced   argued   asked   babbled

barked   bawled   bellowed   bleated

blurted   called   chattered   cheered

croaked   drawled   growled   grumbled

hissed   muttered   piped   quavered

ranted   roared   shouted   stammered

snapped   sobbed   whimpered   sighed

There's nothing wrong with using the word said.

BUT I LIKE TO YELL!

And I like to whisper.

Handwriting: fluency and legibility; all joins. **Grammar**: saying verbs. **Spelling and vocabulary**: synonyms. **Literary elements**: words for said.

Interjections are words that show emotion or feelings. They can stand alone.

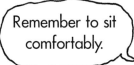

Remember to sit comfortably.

Trace then write the interjection for each emotion.
Write an interjection in each speech bubble.

angry: grrr agh humph

happy: bravo eureka yippee

sad: aw alas drat

worried: uh oh oops oh no

questioning: hey eh huh

scared: eek ahhhh yikes

relieved: phew golly whoa

Handwriting: fluency and legibility; all joins. **Grammar**: interjections.

Trace the nouns for items in the kitchen. Then, for each letter of the alphabet, write your own noun for something in your home.

almonds   bok choy   curry   dumplings

a   b   c   d

eggflip   forks   garbage   herbs

e   f   g   h

ice   juice   knives   lemons

i   j   k   l

mangos   nuts   oranges   plates

m   n   o   p

quinces   radishes   sausages   tangerines

q   r   s   t

utensils   vegetables watermelon

u   v   w

mixer   yoghurt   zucchinis

x   y   z

(Self-assessment) Circle five words that show your writing is fluent and legible.

Handwriting: fluency and legibility; all joins. **Grammar:** nouns. **Spelling and vocabulary:** different types of plurals -es (radishes), -s (lemons), no change from singular to plural (bok choy, garbage, ice, yoghurt).

Remember to keep your letter shape, size, slope and spacing consistent.

Trace then write.

Thomas sat in the doctor's waiting room,

trying not to panic about his arm.

It wasn't looking good. A red stain

was seeping through the bandage.

Oops, thought Thomas. I think I used

too much jam.

Self-assessment Cross out the words that don't apply.

I need to work on my letter shapes, slope, spacing, size, tails.

Handwriting: fluency and legibility; all joins. **Grammar:** thinking verbs (thought, think); apostrophe for possession (doctor's); proper noun (Thomas). **Spelling and vocabulary:** apostrophe for contraction (wasn't); homophone (too/to/two). **Literary elements:** third person narrative; point of view; quote from *Doubting Thomas*, by Morris Gleitzman (2006).

Remember to pause if you need to, and relax your hold on the pen or pencil.

Trace then write.

sch school scr scream spl splat

spr sprint shr shriek sph sphere

squ square str straight thr through

Find and write a word of your own for each letter cluster.

sch   scr   spl

spr   shr   sph

squ   str   thr

Trace then write.

Characters in scary movies

shriek and scream.

Screeee

Put a cross next to any joins that you could improve.

Handwriting: fluency and legibility; all joins. **Spelling and vocabulary:** three letter consonant blends 'spl', 'spr', 'scr', 'str'.

31

Trace then write

au automatic aw awful or short sport

ai straight ay day slay ea meat cheat

ee cheek ei eight er germ oa boat oath

ow power shower eu eureka ew drew

ey prey grey ie pie die oi toil boil

oo scoot ou shout oy boy

Eureka

Write words that rhyme.

port	plea	flew
stay	lie	spoil

Handwriting: fluency and legibility, all joins. **Spelling and vocabulary:** digraphs for vowel sounds 'au', 'ai', 'oi', 'ea', 'ee', 'oa', 'ei', 'ie', 'eu', 'ou', 'oo', 'aw', 'or', 'er', 'ew', 'ow', 'ey', 'ay', 'oy'.

Trace then write.

first second third fourth fifth sixth

seventh eighth ninth tenth hundredth

tle castle dge dodge ght night flight

nk stink tion nation lk stalk talk

Choose a homophone from the box for each word below.

| whale | would | know | eight | flower | through | hair |
| creak | steel | boy | choose | fur | stalk | piece | sale |

peace	steal	no
ate	wood	hare
wail	flour	creek
threw	buoy	chews
fir	stork	sail

Handwriting: fluency and legibility; all joins. **Spelling and vocabulary:** homophones; letter patterns -tle, -tion, -ght, -dge, -nk, -lk.

Consolidation: Fluency and legibility

Trace. Then choose a prefix from the box to write an antonym beside each word.

un im ir dis

possible   practical

natural   obedient

rational   mature

approve   regular

intentional

Trace. Then add a suffix from the box to each word. Some words might be able to use more than one suffix.

ful less able

hope   care

effort   waste

wish   thought

dread   approach

fear   answer

Trace these words with silent letters.

thumb   scene   gnaw

knock   autumn   whistle

guitar   guess   wrestle

Handwriting: fluency and legibility; all joins. **Spelling and vocabulary:** antonyms; negative prefixes (um-, im-, ir-, dis-); suffixes (-ful, -less, -able); silent letters (thum<u>b</u>, s<u>c</u>ene, <u>g</u>naw, <u>k</u>nock, autum<u>n</u>, whistle, g<u>u</u>itar, g<u>u</u>ess, <u>w</u>restle).

34

Take care with all your joins.

A **pangram** is a sentence that uses every letter of the alphabet. You can use letters more than once.

Trace then write these pangrams.

The wolf just kept dozing very

quietly in a crumpled box.

The mad taxi driver wove quickly

past the frisky zebra crossing the road.

A big funky ox squashed

the very cute jumping frogs

as they did a waltz.

Self-assessment Cross out the words that don't apply.
I need to work on my letter shapes, slope, spacing, size, tails.

Handwriting: fluency and legibility; all joins. **Literary elements:** pangrams.

Consolidation: Fluency and legibility

Trace then write these sentences about classic stories.

The children entered Narnia through

a wardrobe in the spare room.

A cyclone whirled Dorothy

and Toto to the Land of Oz.

Gulliver was washed ashore in Lilliput.

Peter Pan flew to Neverland.

Alice fell into a rabbit-hole

and discovered Wonderland.

Make sure your writing arm and hand can move freely. Keep your pencil or pen hold relaxed and flexible.

Handwriting: fluency and legibility; all joins. **Grammar:** proper nouns (Narnia, Dorothy, Toto, Land of Oz, Gulliver, Lilliput, Peter Pan, Neverland, Alice, Wonderland); prepositional phrases (through a wardrobe, in the spare room); verbs (whirled, was washed). **Literary elements:** fantasy genre, characters and settings; entering fantasy worlds; references to *The Lion, the Witch and the Wardrobe*, by C S Lewis (1950), *The Wonderful Wizard of Oz*, by L Frank Baum (1900), *Gulliver's Travels*, by Jonathan Swift (1726), *Peter Pan*, by JM Barrie (1911), *Alice's Adventures in Wonderland*, by Lewis Carroll (1865). (Note, these books have all been made into films.)

Trace then write the similes.

as scarce as hen's teeth

as bold as brass

as clear as mud

Trace then write the lines from a playscript.
Scene: Shaggy man and Button-bright face the Scoodlers.

Shaggy man: What do you want?

Scoodlers (yelling, pointing): You!

Shaggy man: What do you want us for?

Scoodlers (shouting): Soup!

Button-bright: Don't want to be soup.

Handwriting: fluency and legibility; all joins. **Grammar:** questions; exclamation; statement; proper nouns (Shaggy man, Scoodlers, Button-bright).
Punctuation: colons; brackets; exclamation marks; question marks. **Literary elements:** similes; tongue-in-cheek humour; irony; colloquialism; stage directions; characters; playscript adapted from Chapter 9, 'Facing the Scoodlers', from *The Road to Oz*, by L Frank Baum (1909).

Some words used in English are of Australian Aboriginal origins.

Trace then write these words for plants and animals.

kangaroo bogong wallaroo wallaby

galah currawong bunyip boobook bilby

quokka quoll waratah myall quandong

yabby kookaburra

wobbegong numbat

brolga taipan dingo

budgerigar mallee wombat witchetty

mulga potoroo koala drongo pademelon

Handwriting: fluency and legibility; all joins. **Spelling and vocabulary:** etymology; words in English from Aboriginal languages.

Writing that all has the same slope looks neater and is easier to read.

An **anagram** is a word or phrase made by changing the order of the letters in another word or phrase.

Trace then write the anagrams.

astronomers = no more stars

conversation = voices rant on

mummy = my mum

the eyes = they see

the countryside = no city dust here

twelve plus one = eleven plus two

Self-assessment   My writing slopes in the same direction:
sometimes ☐   often ☐   always ☐ .

Handwriting: fluency and legibility; all joins; consistent slope. **Literary elements**: anagrams.

Trace then write.

said

he

she

they

his

her

their

your

can

could

from

where

when

which

who

what

These words are from a list of 100 most used words that make up about half of all reading and writing.

You'll need to write these words often. Practise writing them as quickly as you can while still being neat.

(Self-assessment) On each line: Draw a star above the word you wrote the fastest. Tick the word you wrote the neatest.

Handwriting: fluency and legibility; all joins; speed. **Spelling and vocabulary**: common words.

Trace the sentences. Finish each sentence by writing a character name from the box on the next line.

| Rapunzel Goldilocks The Wolf Jack Baby Bear |

"Oh! Someone ate my porridge," cried

"I'll blow your house down," shouted

"Oops! I broke the chair," said

"I'll hang down my hair," said

"Yikes! The Giant is coming!" yelled

Write a sentence of your own for one of the characters in the box.

| Cinderella The Little Mermaid Red Riding Hood Aladdin |

The end.

Handwriting: fluency and legibility; all joins. **Grammar:** interjections; exclamations; dialogue; saying verbs (cried, shouted, yelled, said); proper nouns (Goldilocks, Cinderella, Aladdin). **Punctuation:** speech marks; exclamation marks; apostrophe for contraction (I'll). **Literary elements:** fairy tales; story characters.

41

Trace then write. Finish the speech bubbles.

The gnome made fudge on Wednesday.

He had to guard the dessert from the

naughty knight at the castle, so he

climbed a cliff and hid it under some

thistles. He ate the fudge after an hour,

leaving no crumbs.

I have a
toothache.

Handwriting: fluency and legibility; all joins. **Spelling and vocabulary:** words with silent letters (gnome, Wednesday, guard, naughty, knight, castle, climbed, thistles, hour, crumbs); fudge uses dge to make a j sound; desert/dessert often confused. **Literary elements:** fantasy characters (gnome, knight, dragon).

Practise making your f's fluent.

Trace then write an anagram for each word.

flee   fringe

fits   file

fowl   softer

cafe   fare

framed   flea

Trace then write.

The fly flitted through fifty flowers.

Four friends ate fresh, fried, fly fritters.

Five frantic frogs fled from fierce fishes.

Handwriting: fluency and legibility; f. **Literary elements:** anagrams; alliteration; tongue twisters.

43

Make sure you write neatly so others can read your writing.

Trace then write.

A fly and flea flew into a flue,

said the fly to the flea,

"What shall we do?"

"Let us fly," said the flea.

Said the fly, "Shall we flee?"

So they flew through

a flaw in the flue.

Self-assessment Circle your five best joins on this page.

Handwriting: fluency and legibility; f. **Grammar**: sentences; questions. **Punctuation**: speech marks; commas; question marks. **Literary elements**: alliteration; tongue twisters.

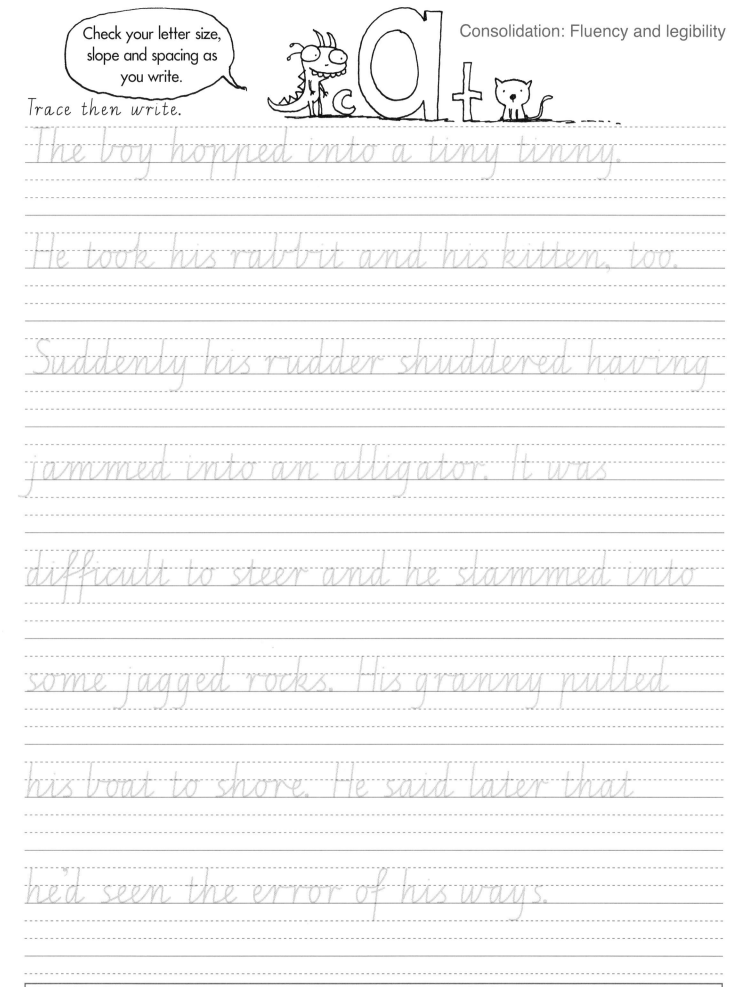

Check your letter size, slope and spacing as you write.

Trace then write.

The boy hopped into a tiny tinny.

He took his rabbit and his kitten, too.

Suddenly his rudder shuddered having

jammed into an alligator. It was

difficult to steer and he slammed into

some jagged rocks. His granny pulled

his boat to shore. He said later that

he'd seen the error of his ways.

Handwriting: fluency and legibility; double letters ee, dd, ff, ll, mm, nn, oo, rr, bb, gg, pp. **Spelling and vocabulary:** common mistakes (tiny/tinny, hopped/hoped); rhyme (rudder/shudder, slammed/jammed).

Consolidation: Fluency and legibility

Trace then write this stanza from a Henry Lawson poem.

It leapt across the flaming streams

And raced the pastures through;

It climbed the trees, and lit the boughs,

And fierce and fiercer grew.

The bees fell stifled in the smoke

Or perished in their hives,

And with the stock the kangaroos

Went flying for their lives.

Handwriting: fluency and legibility, all joins. **Spelling and vocabulary:** 'ough' (through, bough). **Literary elements:** quote from 'The Fire at Ross's Farm', published in *The Days When The World Was Wide*, by Henry Lawson (1900).

Choose one of the limericks. Write it in your best joined writing. Draw an illustration for it.

There was an old man in a barge,
Whose nose was exceedingly large;
But in fishing by night, it supported a light,
Which helped that old man in a barge.

There was a young lady of Greenwich,
Whose garments were border'd with Spinach;
But a large spotty Calf bit her shawl quite in half,
Which alarmed that young lady of Greenwich.

Handwriting: fluency and legibility; all joins. **Grammar:** possessive pronoun (whose). **Punctuation:** capital to start each line of a poem; semicolons. **Literary elements:** limericks; 'There Was an Old Man in a Barge', and 'There was a Young Lady of Greenwich', from *More Nonsense, Pictures, Rhymes, Botany &c*, by Edward Lear (1872).

Complete the crime scene report to investigate what happened to Humpty Dumpty. Did Humpty fall or was it foul play?

When you fill in a form, it sometimes says you have to complete the form in block letters. This means you have to use all capital letters.

CRIME SCENE REPORT
TO BE COMPLETED IN BLOCK LETTERS

TYPE OF CRIME	
WHERE CRIME TOOK PLACE	
TIME CRIME TOOK PLACE	
VICTIM DETAILS	
DESCRIPTION OF CRIME SCENE	
EVIDENCE COLLECTED	
WITNESS NAME	
WITNESS STATEMENT	

Handwriting: capitals. Literary elements: common expression (foul play).

Here is a new script to use for printing labels in projects, maps and other displays.

Notice there are no rounded entries on m, n or r. Look at the crossbar on f.

Trace then write.

a b c d e f g h i j k l m

n o p q r s t u v w x y z

Trace then write.

"Oooh! Oooh!" exclaimed the owl.

"What did you say?" asked the robin.

Wise

?

Handwriting: introducing new print script. **Grammar:** statement; question; sentence. **Punctuation:** capital letters to start sentences; full stop; question mark; exclamation mark.

Print script for labelling

Trace then write.

A wise old owl sat in an oak.

The more he heard the less he spoke.

The less he spoke the more he heard.

Why aren't we all like that wise old bird?

Notice there are no exits on a d h i l m n o t or u.

Trace the capital. Then write the matching lower-case letter.

A B C D E F

G H I J K L

M N O P Q R

S T U V W X

Y Z

Handwriting: introducing new print script. **Grammar:** statement; question; sentence. **Punctuation:** capital letters to start sentences; full stop; question mark; exclamation mark. **Spelling and vocabulary:** rhyme (heard/bird, oak/spoke). **Literary elements:** Mother Goose rhyme.

Some place names in Australia come from Australian Aboriginal languages.

Print the labels on the map.

1 Mundaring
2 Karratha
3 Pilbara
4 Jabiru
5 Kalgoorlie
6 Coolgardie
7 Yulara
8 Nhulunbuy
9 Aurukun
10 Tanunda
11 Cocklebiddy
12 Biloela
13 Noosa
14 Maroochydore
15 Currumbin
16 Arakoon
17 Wilcannia
18 Dubbo
9 Uralla
20 Turramurra
21 Parramatta
22 Ballarat
23 Thirroul
24 Geelong
25 Wonthaggi
26 Canberra

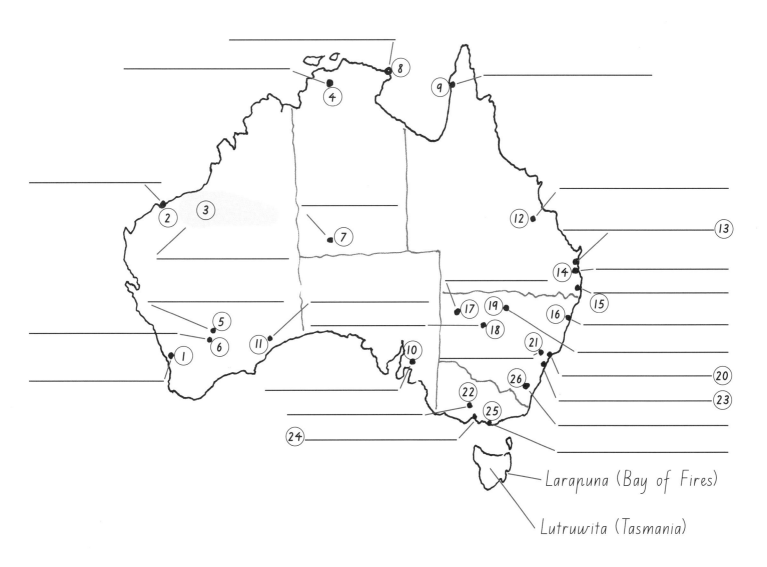

Larapuna (Bay of Fires)

Lutruwita (Tasmania)

Handwriting: using print script to label maps. **Spelling and vocabulary:** etymology; Aboriginal languages.

Print script for labelling

1 Pick a genre.

scary ☐   adventure ☐   historical ☐

mystery ☐   fantasy ☐   funny ☐

2 Draw a map of a possible setting for a story in your chosen genre.

3 Add labels. Include labels to describe what you might see, hear, smell, feel and taste if you were standing in this setting.

Remember to use print script for labels.

Self-assessment   My print script on this page is:
improving ☐ good ☐ fantastic ☐.

Handwriting: print script for labels on maps and diagrams. Literary elements: genre; setting; descriptions.

Choose an adjective and a noun for each label. Remember to use print script.

Adjectives	awesome, fearsome, loathsome, cumbersome, troublesome, handsome, gruesome
Nouns	teeth, jaws, scales, legs, tail, claws, eyes

Label any extra parts you like. Give the creature a name.

- -

- -

- -

Handwriting: using print script to label diagrams. **Grammar:** adjectives; nouns; noun groups. **Spelling and vocabulary:** suffix -some.
Literary elements: mythical creatures (dragons, beasts).

g g g

Write the   Take the tail up   and cross the letter's
letter.   at a 45° angle . . .   tail at the baseline.

The letters g j y and z end with their tails facing left. Speedloops can help you to join them.

Write the letters.

g   g   g   ga   ge   gi   go   gr   gu

y   y   y   ya   ye   yi   yo   yu   ya

Write the anagram pairs.

garden danger   grin ring   yap pay

Write the tongue twister.

Granny has a grey

goose that gets grumpy.

Handwriting: introducing speed loops from tail letters (descenders) g, j, y, and z. **Literary elements:** anagrams; alliteration; tongue twisters.

Speed loops help you to connect letters by the quickest means, so loops should be small.

Loops should only be half the letter's body width.

Write the letters.

j   j   j   ja   je   ji   jo   ju   ja

z   z   z   za   ze   zi   zo   zu   zo

Write the words.

zoot   zoom   zippy   zesty   daze

zany   tizzy   fizzy   dizzy   haze

Write the words.

jam   jammed   jest   jeer

juggernaut   joyous   journey

There's no need to loop at the end of word. But you can if it helps your fluency.

Self-assessment   My speedloops cross at the baseline:
sometimes ☐   often ☐   always ☐.

Handwriting: introducing speed loops from tail letters (descenders) g, j, y, and z. **Spelling and vocabulary:** rhyme; alliteration.

a   *a'*   *al*

Take the exit stroke up at a 45° angle . . .

then go left to make a loop.

Cross the loop at the top body line and finish the letter.

Speed loops help with fluency and speed because they reduce the need for retracing.

Write the letter pairs. Try using speed loops.

ab ah al eh el ib ik il ob

ol ub uh ul dl rl tl wl

You don't need a loop on b, h, k or l at the start of a word.

Write the anagram pairs.

lump plum   *bruise rubies*

horse shore   *weak wake*

pastel staple   *please elapse*

Self-assessment   My speedloops cross at the top body line:
sometimes ☐   often ☐   always ☐ .

Handwriting: speed loops to head and body letters (ascenders) b, h, k and l. **Literary elements**: anagrams.

Write.

gl gl gl glow glee glare gloom

gh gh gh light fright might tight

sight delight polite height bludge

babble dabble sobbed robbed

Write the tongue twister.

She sells sea shells by the sea shore.

The shells she sells are seashells, I'm sure.

Handwriting: speed loops to head and body letters (ascenders) b, h, k and l. **Spelling and vocabulary**: rhyme. **Literary elements**: tongue twisters.

57

Write.

Peter Piper picked a peck

of pickled peppers.

A peck of pickled peppers

Peter Piper picked.

If Peter Piper picked a peck

of pickled peppers,

where's the peck of pickled peppers

Peter Piper picked?

Speed loops need less pressure than downstrokes. So lighten up on your pencil if making loops.

Self-assessment My handwriting style is:

improving ☐ good ☐ fantastic ☐.

Handwriting: developing a personal style which is legible, fluent, easy to maintain and aesthetically pleasing. **Literary elements**: tongue twisters.

You do not have to use speed loops. Only use them if they help you to write faster and if your writing is still legible.

Write.

In the High and Far-Off Times the

Elephant, O Best Beloved, had no

trunk. He had only a blackish,

bulgy nose, as big as a boot, that he

could wriggle about from side to side;

but he couldn't pick up things with it.

Self-assessment Rate your writing out of 10:
fluency ___ speed ___ legibility ___ .

Handwriting: developing a personal style which is legible, fluent, easy to maintain and aesthetically pleasing. **Literary elements**: simile (as big as a boot); quote from 'The Elephant's Child' from *Just So Stories*, by Rudyard Kipling (1902).

A signature needs to be the same each time you write it. It needs to be quick and easy to write.

Experiment with different ways to sign your name.

Choose your favourite signature. Practise writing it on the lines.
Try to write each signature exactly the same.

Self-assessment   Circle your favourite signature.

Handwriting: developing a personal style which is legible, fluent, easy to maintain and aesthetically pleasing; developing a signature.

Collect autographs from your classmates and teachers.

An autograph is someone's signature.

You can stamp and rage,
I'm still first on this page.

You'd better write fast,
or you'll be the last!

61

Have a classmate time you as you rewrite the sentence from the box. Use all the joins you have learned. Make sure you write as fluently and legibly as you can.

Grumpy dancers caught a quick taxi to Wonthaggi to juggle volleyballs for the crazy human circus.

Assessment 1

Date _____   Time _____ minutes _____ seconds

Assessment 2

Date _____   Time _____ minutes _____ seconds

Assessment 3

Date _____   Time _____ minutes _____ seconds

Assessment 4

Date _____   Time _____ minutes _____ seconds

Handwriting: writing quickly but with fluency and legibility. **Grammar:** adjectives (grumpy, quick); classifying adjective (human); common nouns (dancers, volleyball, taxi, circus); proper noun (Wonthaggi); action verbs (caught, juggle). **Literary elements:** pangram.

Read each of the criteria listed below. When you think you have achieved each one, write the date and sign off.

My letters are consistently the right shape and an even size. ☐ _____

My letters are a consistent height. ☐ _____

My letters sit on the base line correctly. ☐ _____

My letter tails hang down correctly. ☐ _____

My letters have the same slope. ☐ _____

The space between my letters is regular. ☐ _____

The space between my words is regular. ☐ _____

My joins are fluent. ☐ _____

Others can easily read my joined handwriting. ☐ _____

My writing is automatic. (I don't have to think too hard about how to join the letters fluently.) ☐ _____

I can write quickly when I need to and my fast writing is legible to others. ☐ _____

I have started to develop my own personal handwriting style. ☐ _____

Have you signed off on each of the criteria? You've successfully completed your journey to the worlds of FLUENCY and LEGIBILITY.

Congratulations!